ANGELS OF LIGHT

5

Five Spiritualists
test the spirits

40 Beansburn, Kilmarnock, Scotland

Contents

Chap.	Title	Author	Pg.
Intro			**3**
1.	**Seance Fever**	*Ben Alexander*	**4**
2.	**Set Free**	*Sadie Bryce*	**11**
3.	**Enticed by the Light**	*Dr. Sharon Beekmann*	**17**
4.	**Saved out of Spiritualism**	*Jackie Lancaster*	**24**
5.	**The Beautiful Side of Evil**	*Johanna Michaelsen*	**28**
6.	**For the Reader**		**48**

Introduction

Spiritualism is an ancient practice known to people of every culture and nation, which includes attempting to communicate with the dead, psychic healing and various other supernatural activities.

Today spiritualism is experiencing explosive growth, particularly in the West, with many millions dabbling in it or dedicated to it worldwide.

This booklet contains the life-stories of five mediums who were all deeply involved in spiritualism. They take us on an incredible journey.

CHAPTER 1

Seance Fever

Ben Alexander
Former Spiritualist Medium

My childhood in the 1920's and 30's in England left much to be desired. After all that my mother endured from my cruel and merciless father, it is little wonder I found her, on more than one occasion, having taken an overdose to escape the misery. My childhood trauma was heightened one night when I awoke to hear my father screaming;

"*I don't want to die; I'm going to hell."*

He passed away the next morning. Not many years later my mother died. Despite my upbringing in the Jewish faith, being left an orphan at so young an age had a profound effect on me. Although I was sent to a Hebrew School and taught the faith of my fathers I rebelled. The older I grew the less all the 'religious stuff' meant to me.

As a grown man I turned to pleasure and worldly pursuits. Sadly, it was not long before I found myself the slave of various evil habits. Eventually becoming desperate I began a search for God. Despite my earnest cry for help, "*God, if you are there please help me,*" my prayers seemed to go unanswered. My search included reading up on the world's major religions and cults. I studied the teachings of everything from the Jehovah's Witnesses to Hinduism and yoga, but I never found what I was looking for. In a strange way I could hardly have explained what I really was looking for. I suppose it was the 'answer to life', or simply inner peace. How illusive it was.

Then I seemed to see light at the end of the tunnel. I met a spiritualist medium. She told me, with great earnestness and in all seriousness, that she had contacted many from the spirit world. Excited and fascinated by this new and mysterious information, I eagerly investigated and soon began to take part in many forms of spiritualism. This included ESP, clairvoyance, healing, ouija boards, automatic writing, psychokinesis, trumpet speaking, psychometry, trance and transfiguration. Yet for all this, the joy and peace for which I so deeply longed did not materialise. Instead, I found that my married life became a living hell of constant bickering and arguing. I was sick and tired of my marital relationship. For comfort I turned all the more to spiritualism. In fact, it now dominated my life.

In 1956 my wife and I went to the USA. While there we became friends with a lovely Christian family. After a year we returned to England. Unknown to me, the family we met in the USA started to pray for my wife and me from that point on. Back home again, I became more and more embedded in spiritualism.

While moving in spiritualist circles I met some interesting and powerful characters. A mother and son in particular fascinated me. They invited me to a seance one evening, promising spectacular manifestations. That evening, before we began, I took the opportunity to examine the room in which the seance was to be held. There are plenty of phonies in the spiritualist world. One cannot afford to blindly accept everything without a thorough investigation. As the seance began the son went into a trance. A substance called ectoplasm began to flow out of his nose and mouth. Of its own accord a cone-shaped trumpet that lay on the floor began to rise. Spirits spoke through this trumpet. Later a spirit appeared, its shape formed by the ectoplasm. *"Welcome back Ben. We missed you,"* the spirit said.

I was excited by this powerful experience. This must be the answer to life after death, I thought. As we continued attending more and more seances, sometimes we used the Bible and prayed over it in the hope of bringing forth greater phenomena. Suddenly the Bible would rise and slam against the wall. It was as though someone had thrown it away in anger.

"This was done because there was an evil spirit present," reassured a spirit. *"But we good spirits will see to it that it doesn't happen again."*

But it did happen again - many times. By this stage I was totally enthralled. What a privilege to have God speak directly to me through His spirits. I became helplessly obsessed with a desire for greater and greater manifestations. However, I soon received more than I expected. Nightmares! Oh, those awful nightmares - and that overwhelming fear. Dogged by horrible manifestations, I fled from my spiritualist mentors and vowed never to return.

I moved away and organised my own seance circle. Acting as a medium gave me a great sense of power. In my mind I thought, *"I shall be the greatest mediator ever, between God's spiritual world and the physical world."* However, success in the spiritualist world was not mirrored by success at home. My marriage crumbled beneath me. I remarried and moved again to the USA. My wife and I hoped to start a spiritualist centre in America. My one close acquaintance in America was the Christian family I had met previously. We decided to visit them. During the course of our visit I suggested a trip to their church. I was hoping I might be able to influence some of our friends' church associates to join our spiritualist organisation. As I went to the meeting of the church the following Sunday, I was struck by the friendliness of the people. I settled down to listen to the sermon.

The preacher said something that startled me; in fact it was a quotation from the Bible. He said;

"*Though your sins are as scarlet, they shall be as white as snow.*"

As he continued, he stressed that freedom from fear, guilt and sin could be mine if I would repent and receive Jesus Christ as Lord and Saviour. This struck a chord in my heart. How I longed for peace and the forgiveness of my sins.

I went back for the night meeting. That night they were having an evening of singing. As they loudly and joyfully sang the songs about the Saviour and how He died on the cross and rose again from the dead, I couldn't help thinking;

"*These people have something I don't have.*"

I longed for rest and peace - but how? I stood up and went to the front of the building while the singing continued. I wanted to speak to the preacher.

He took me into an office and bluntly asked me;

"*Ben, have you received Jesus as your Lord and Saviour?*"

I admitted I hadn't. The preacher put before me again the offer of full forgiveness through the death and resurrection of the Son of God, the Lord Jesus. I told him my sins were too great to be forgiven.

For a full hour we wrestled through all my past, my preconceived notions and my fears. Finally, I clearly understood that I was a lost sinner and that hell would be my destiny unless I repented and received the Lord. That moment I turned from my sin and, believing that Christ died for me, I knelt and asked God to save my soul. According to the promises in the Bible and true to His word, God forgave me that day on the basis of the sacrifice of His only Son. Oh, what peace and joy flooded into my heart! I was a new person. The past had gone and my sins had been forgiven.

A few days later, not knowing about God's condemnation of seances, a great battle for my soul took place while holding a seance. The Lord was prompting me in my mind saying, *"This is an abomination to your God, Ben. Have no more to do with this work of Satan."* On the other side were the spirits, now in their true colour as demons saying *"Don't listen to Him, Ben. You can have great knowledge and power to rule others."* In my anguish I cried out, *"Stop! No longer will I have anything to do with the spirits of darkness."*

I broke all my contacts with my spiritualist associates. I put my heart into studying the Bible. I came to the realisation that all the spirits connected with spiritualism are evil, despite their impressive claims to be 'good'. These spirits are angels, who along with Satan attempted to overthrow God's kingdom and were cast out of heaven. They became evil spirits who are now well able to deceive by impersonation and manifestation. They are powerful and malicious, but they wear a cloak of beauty and charm.

But if spiritualism is evil, how and why do mediums cast out evil spirits and do good works? The answer is very simple, as another ex-medium once explained. The Devil is most certainly not casting out demons, neither is his house divided, neither are those spirits 'good spirits'. In fact they are all demons. Demons have to use some method of deception in their attempt to prove the counterfeit is really of God, so they play a game of make-believe. Although they are all evil spirits, one pretends to be a good spirit while another plays the part of a bad one. The evil spirit starts first, finding no difficulty in cursing and swearing and taking great care that he does not overcome the team of workers too often, occasionally pretending to be mastered by them. The act is well planned.

On the other hand, the other demon is acting as a good spirit, professing to be highly evolved and able to deal with bad spirits for their own good. The so-called good spirit speaks to the evil spirit, who at first appears to be antagonistic, but eventually obeys orders and they both trot off together, to laugh at the credulity of human nature that makes it possible for such a hoax to be played out.

Since the Bible is so clearly against all contact with the departed, how do we account for the phenomena that take place in modern spiritualistic seances? Sir. Oliver Lodge and Sir. Arthur Conan Doyle were both men of renown and there is no reason to doubt that their statements are true, so far as facts are concerned. The conclusions they drew from these 'facts' are another matter entirely.

Consider the following argument:

(1) Either God now permits that which He once forbade and condemned or;

(2) The evil spirits are at the root of all the messages received. Thus, contact is not made with the departed dead, but with the demons impersonating them.

If (1) were true these messages would have to be in complete harmony with the Scriptures and the Lord Jesus Christ would be exalted far above all else. However, as many spiritualists will admit, the messages received are often not in agreement with the Bible at all.

If (2) is true, what sort of message would the listener at the seance expect to receive? Naturally one of comfort and consolation to overcome the anxiety and worry of the one left behind. With all fear of the future gone, and death explained as only a natural process of evolution, there is no need for those left behind to take the Bible seriously when it warns us that it is appointed unto men once to die but after death the judgment.

If we accept the Bible's warnings of judgment we must make a definite decision and take our stand in this life, for Christ. But if we can do away with this belief for the time being, it will be too late after death to seek the grace and salvation of God, and Satan has grasped another soul to accompany him to the fire "prepared for the devil and his angels". To accomplish this purpose, the spirits will tell the listener that their loved ones are perfectly happy on the other side of life, that suffering is non-existent, and all this in spite of the beliefs they once held - or did not hold - with regard to Almighty God and the salvation He has provided.

In order to remove all doubt from the mind of the enquirer, the evil spirit usually shows some intimate knowledge of the person being impersonated. The listener is quickly assured and convinced that the 'spirit' is really and truly the spirit of their dearly departed loved one. But this kind of knowledge is easily accessible for a demon. Then, having removed all worry and anxiety, and having gained the confidence of the troubled relative, the demon will then speak concerning religion and Christianity. Satan knows the scriptures better than any human. He is a master at 'quoting the Bible' – but always with a subtle twist, thus deceiving the unwary. In spite of the fact that spiritualists often quote Scriptures as a basis for their doctrines and arguments, it is to be noted that these quotations are only fragments of the Scriptures, most often taken out of context without reference to the sound doctrines that arise from a serious spiritual study of the word of God as a whole.

As one who was heavily involved in the spiritualist scene for many years, let me assure the reader that what I say is the result of first hand knowledge of one of the cleverest deceptions on the earth today.

CHAPTER 2

Set Free

Sadie Bryce
Glasgow, Scotland

I am no theologian; just an ordinary Glasgow housewife. In fact, to go back to my origins, I was born a Geordie in Newcastle upon Tyne. The only name on my birth certificate was 'Sadie'.

A childhood visit from my grandparents changed my life. They arrived to find me black and blue and decided to take me home with them to Glasgow in Scotland. I fell in love with Glasgow and at the age of 19 married one of Glasgow's 'lovely guys'. Despite being parted for a while during the Second World War, we had a truly happy marriage and were blessed with one daughter, Helena.

There always seemed to be one day too many for the money each week and many times we had to magically turn one potato into a plate of chips between us. My first real 'knock' came when my husband visited the doctor complaining of a pain in his leg. He was diagnosed with secondary cancer - too far gone to do anything. Although they told him he'd pull through and soon be back on his feet, they took me into a small room and told me he had five months to live.

The only life I had known up to that point centred on my husband and home. That was now shattered. What was I to do? I had no church connection or religious faith of any kind. I carried on the illusion, not telling my husband the truth about his cancer. It soon developed into 24 hour round the clock care. As predicted, five months later he died at home. I had to find a minister to conduct the funeral. It was terrible. During the year that followed all I wanted to do was to commit suicide and just opt out of life. At night I would just put my coat on and walk up and down the Great Western Road not knowing what I was doing or where I was going. I was a lost soul in more ways than one.

After a year I realised I was so selfishly wrapped up in *my* loss that I had neglected my own daughter. She had lost a father after all. It was time to pull myself together. The library became a source of comfort to me. I read and read - and the one type of book I was constantly drawn to was about spiritualism. Each book presented the 'proof' for spiritualism and I began to seriously wonder was there anything in it? I began to feel I was being 'led' to these books. They didn't frighten me; rather they fascinated me.

Then one Sunday morning I went to visit a friend to comfort her on the loss of her husband. As we chatted together she said;

"I have heard that you can get in touch with the dead."

"Yes," I replied. *"I have heard that. I've read a couple of books on the subject."*

My friend went on to explain how to use a ouija board. We decided to give it a go - and it worked! This fed my fascination all the more. Then one evening I picked up the Evening Newspaper and read the churches' column. There, alongside the usual Christian churches was a notice about the local spiritualist church. Immediately I had a tremendous urge to go there. Without delay I put on my coat and headed for this spiritualist church. All apprehension was removed as I walked into the building. It looked just like a normal church to me. I was even handed a hymn book as I entered. The 'service' started with a prayer in which they called upon God to help them to contact the spirits. The experience was very real to me. Through one spiritualist on the platform I was given a message, supposedly from my husband, and I believed it. The medium projected my husband's very personality and character in what she said. I just knew it was my husband. I had known him more closely than anyone for many years - I couldn't be deceived - it was definitely him.

I became a dedicated attendee at this spiritualist church which was one of the main centres of spiritualism in Scotland. I was amazed at the information the mediums gave out. I never at any time had any fear. As I sat in this 'church' with my hymn book, singing hymns and listening to prayers, I comforted myself with the thought that this whole medium business must be of God.

One day one of the mediums said;

"You're going to be given a gift Sadie. I think it's the gift of healing."

My ego responded to that word of encouragement!

"What," I replied. *"Do you mean I am going to be able to pray for someone and they will be healed?"*

Incredible as it seemed to me, an ordinary Glasgow housewife, I was now given the abilities of clairvoyance and clairaudience. Clairaudience is the ability to hear spirit voices as clearly as if a person were speaking right next to you. My ego was on a high. I remember walking along Argyle Street one day saying to myself;

"Why has God gifted me like this?"

Unworthy thoughts also filled my mind. I thought of all the money I could make in this field and not have to declare it to the Inland Revenue. All unbeknown to me, I had now reached a stage where I had little control over my own life. Around this time, a friend who owned a taxi cab business at Anniesland Cross asked me to do some receptionist work for him. He was desperate for help and I agreed to do the work. I went for an interview with him and his brother. We struck it off well and I agreed to start work the next day.

As I headed home from the interview I stood at the bus stop at Anniesland Cross. In my mind I was beginning to wonder if it was not time to have done with my mediumship and get back to 'normal life' again. No sooner had these thoughts crossed my mind than the spirits within me who had always been friendly, suddenly turned aggressive.

I heard voices within me threatening me with all sorts of disasters if I left spiritualism. I tried to shut the voices out of my head but I was losing the battle. I wanted to scream, but with people either side of me at the bus stop I felt I would probably end up in a mental hospital on drugs, which would have masked my real problem, not cured it.

It was then that God came into my life. He came in with the words of the Lord's Prayer;

"Our Father which art in heaven."

I began to repeat it and when I came to the words *"deliver us from evil"* the turmoil inside me subsided. As I entered the No. 20 bus I was still repeating the words, almost like a magical lucky charm, but with heartfelt sincerity none the less. I held on to the words like grim death. When I reached the multi-story block of flats where I lived and approached my front door on the ninth floor, for the first time in my life I was afraid to put the key in the door. All the memories of my communion with the spirits within the confines of my flat flooded back into my mind.

I plucked up all my courage and entered the flat. I stood in the living room and it was then that I knew fear like I had never known in my life. I wanted to run for help. I thought of my neighbours. No, they wouldn't understand. What about my doctor? I thought about him giving me a prescription and asking me to come back in two weeks time. I knew that wasn't the answer. Then I thought about the church. But it was 7 O'clock at night and it was winter. I could see the church all closed up with the gates locked. How would I find the minister on a night like this?

Perhaps it was a good thing I didn't find any Christians that night. They would no doubt have told me I was demon possessed and in need of deliverance. While they would have been correct, that would not have helped me. It would have driven me away. As I faced my predicament in the flat that night, I began to wonder what the real source of my clairvoyancy was. Like a radio receives 'signals' without wires, so I received messages without 'wires', but from where? Just then God spoke to me. Looking back now I can only put it down to divine intervention. In my mind I felt God saying to me;

"Put all these things away from you, they are an abomination in my sight."

I was directed to all the spiritualist magazines lying round the house. I picked them up, tore them in pieces and put them in the kitchen bin. I was a fifty-four year old spiritualist medium but the Lord seemed to lead me like a child to my daughter's bedroom at the end of the hall where lay a copy of my mother-in-law's Bible. With the Bible in my hands, I threw myself down at the side of my bed on my knees and for the first time in my life I cried out to the living God. I simply said;

"Help me, please help me. I don't know what all these things are that are happening all around me. Please help me."

It seemed that the presence of the Lord filled the room. Then I prayed a simple prayer that God seemed to put in my mouth and which reconciled me to Him;

"Father, forgive me, I know I have walked in wrong ways."

The peace of God flooded my soul. I knew God had come into my life. Calling Him Father shocked me. I had been born illegitimate and at age 21 had finally found my birth certificate with the simple word 'Sadie' on it. But now I had a true loving heavenly Father, and I was His daughter!

The Lord showed me what I looked like in his presence. Not just my mediumship, but *all* of my sin. I wept as I saw my sinful self - but that day the blood of Jesus Christ cleansed me from it all. I received the Lord Jesus Christ as my own and personal Saviour. I was free at last. Immediately God took away my bad habits. My drink, my 60 cigarettes a day, my clairvoyance and clairaudience. It all went in a moment. I was lost but now I was found.

That night I closed my eyes and fell asleep. I had one of the best night's sleep I had ever had. There seemed to be a battle still raging, but it was one that I didn't have to worry about. I was simply happy that the Lord was my shepherd and that He would be with me. The next day I had a clear out of all my spiritualist paraphernalia.

I now knew the truth and the truth had set me free. Spiritualism had deceived me hook line and sinker. It had been so subtle. Its hymns, prayers and churches had conned me into thinking it was all of God. I am so thankful that I began to question the movement, for only then did the spirits show their true character. If I had never doubted and questioned, I would likely have died under the spell of the spiritualist deception. May God bless this life story to you and lead you into His truth.

CHAPTER 3

Enticed By The Light

Dr. Sharon Beekmann

Dr. Sharon Beekmann led a successful career in psychotherapy in a private clinic in the USA between 1972 and 1985. Her training in psychology had led her to adopt a humanist world-view and she leaned towards New Age thinking in many areas. In 1976, Sharon began a quest into spirituality along with some of her friends. She came across books by Jane Roberts called *Seth Speaks* and *The Nature of Interpersonal Reality*, books apparently written through Jane Roberts' Spirit guide, Seth.

These books captivated Sharon. She recalls: *"I believed that laws governed the spiritual universe and protected me from harm. 'Like attracts like', the authors and leaders said. 'When you seek after truth and love, you attract spiritual energies of a like nature and they empower your journey'. I believed them. I thought that as I pursued spiritual truths, the universe facilitated my development and nothing of a lower or unlike nature could harm me. I first learned these principles while reading the Seth books."*

Sharon discovered that the teachings of the spirit guide Seth were completely compatible with existential philosophy and humanistic theories, but that he took psychology to a deeper level.

Jane Roberts had originally contacted Seth whilst experimenting with a ouija board, so Sharon followed her example and purchased one herself. As she used it she discovered, to her amazement, that a spirit revealed itself and spelt out whole sentences. Apparently the spirit had lived on earth before and it gave details of its previous life. To Sharon this was clear confirmation of the material in Jane Robert's books. It was a kind of hands on validation of the existence of a 'spirit world'.

A week later she contacted and visited John and Donna, the leaders of a spiritualist church. She experienced a supernatural encounter as Donna went into a trance and her spirit guide suggested that Sharon was very talented and should attend the spiritual development classes led by the pastors John and Donna. So it was, Sharon began attending the classes regularly. Eventually Sharon blossomed into a full-blown Spiritualist medium with considerable abilities.

She developed in her psychic ability and progressed to eventually link up with five spirit guides. She continued to learn from her mentor, Donna, who advised her; *"Your task is to get out of the way. We want your mind to be a blank slate to enable spirits to move accurately and convey their images and impressions. Practice clearing your mind and releasing your will as you meditate each morning."*

Sharon writes: *"Finally in 1984, seven years after joining the class, my guides spoke through me. I sat erect but comfortably in a folding chair, breathed deeply and cleared my mind. As a thought came, I gave it no energy and instead looked at the black expanse in my mind's eye. I further released my spirit and entered the twilight place experienced between sleep and wakefulness - fully present but dis-engaged. I waited for guidance.*

"I drifted further away, and as I did, another presence swished into my body, moved my mouth, blinked my eyes, and

exercised the muscles of my face. He talked. I listened from my distant shelf, fully confident I could exercise my right to re-enter my body if I chose. But I saw no need. In a respectful manner, he related positive, uplifting and personally encouraging messages. When the reading ended, he left as quickly as he came, and I became fully myself and present to the person seated across from me."

Sharon's spirit guides came only when invited and left when each session concluded. She never questioned their intentions or character - that is, until January 1985, when the one called Seth turned on her after she refused to communicate material that she thought would frighten people. It was as a result of this that she told her spirit guides that she no longer wanted to be a medium.

Sharon explains; *"I noticed that my life wasn't going very well. The spirits were asking for more of my time and attention, and I was beginning to feel as if my life was not my own. About that time, the spirits asked me to predict that a nuclear holocaust would devastate the planet in the summer of 1987. At first I wrote their discourse down because they had never given me a reason to mistrust them, but the message frightened me, and I knew it would frighten others.*

"Finally I told them that I didn't want to convey the message and that I intended to stop channelling. I really wanted to do more of my own thinking. They seemed disappointed but wished me well. The next morning I awoke consumed by an evil presence. It was an odious spirit. I begged him to leave, but my pleading seemed to make matters worse. Because he was so hard to cope with, I had to close my practice and simply endure his torture. Then in September he let up and I started to work again. My other guides tried to help as best they could."

Then one morning during breakfast, *all* the spirit guides attacked Sharon, even after her many years of faithful service. They turned on her. Up till then they had more or less fooled her with their charade of care and compassion. Now she found they were liars - every one of them evil - and they were controlling her body and mind. She didn't know how to make them leave! Sharon saw through the spiritualist scene. She had reached the point that many mediums reach. The spirits expected total passivity from their host. They would give her a level of peace, but only when she complied with their requests. Because she resisted total control, they began to torture her. Often she would hear the voices jeering in her mind: *"We control what happens here!"*

Sharon considered going to other psychotherapists for help, but she realised that most of them would say they believed her experience was only psychological, not spiritual. She even thought about going to a Jungian therapist but changed her mind when she remembered that Jung himself had developed some of his theories through a spirit guide.

She tried contacting a Pastor of the Unity Church who led study groups in *A Course in Miracles* by Helen Schucman. Schucman claimed that her spirit guide 'Jesus' channelled the messages for her book. However, when Sharon phoned, the Pastor told her to go elsewhere and hung up. Again she was unsuccessful when she contacted the spiritualist minister. He blamed her for not 'focusing on the light' and inviting evil in, but he did not help her. Sharon tried treatment from her friend Molly who used ancient Chinese healing arts on her customers. Despite trying to clear the chakras (supposed energy points in the body) through various techniques, the problem continued.

She even tried joining a group of Sai Baba devotees, to seek deliverance because she had heard that this famous Guru could do many miracles. Again she came away disappointed after persevering for some time. The same was true for a lady who claimed to be a 'Christian' healer. This lady used magic mixed with Christianity to try and drive the evil spirits away from Sharon, but still the spirits remained. She describes how these spirits now began to appear. The spirit 'Jesus', his 'disciples' and every spirit she had ever known would come to her, first in all their splendour and attractiveness, but then as grotesque instruments of evil.

"In an instant I knew an awful truth: for the past ten years I had been duped by evil entities masquerading as spirit guides, counsellors, deceased relatives, saints and angels. They had dazzled me with their prowess and noble thoughts, camouflaging their sadistic nature and sinister designs for my life."

Desperate, Sharon telephoned an old friend called Tad who was also a psychotherapist. Tad had once been a Zen Buddhist but had now become a Christian. She understood what Sharon said as she poured out her heart, and later sent a Bible and a book about how a spiritualist medium had become possessed by spirits but was delivered by Jesus Christ.

When Sharon started reading in the Bible about Jesus' encounter with the devil she was sceptical. *"Devil?"* she thought. *"Does anyone still believe in the devil? And which Jesus are they writing about here anyway? The ascended master of the light, or the one who channelled the course in miracles, or the impostor who torments me, or is this the Jesus of the Mormon Church, the one my mother tried to emulate?"*

Sharon then read the book Tad gave her. It was called *The Beautiful Side of Evil* by Johanna Michaelsen (featured in the last chapter of this book). She was stunned. Here was a spiritualist medium who had gone through the same scenario and torment but who had been freed by the Jesus Christ of the Bible.

Again the spiritual attacks resumed and she tried to deal with them herself until she remembered Johanna's testimony. It was at this point she decided she wanted to turn to Jesus Christ and become a Christian. She telephoned Tad again who advised her to go to a church and tell the preacher that she was demon-possessed and wanted to receive Jesus as her Lord and Saviour. Unfortunately, her first attempt proved unhelpful, as the preacher clearly could not handle the problem. Some churches do not believe in the supernatural!

Finally, after some help from various Christians she went to see a minister in a Presbyterian Church in 1987. The minister explained to her clearly that human beings are separated from God by rebellion against Him and His ways. She discovered that religion and moral effort are worthless to restore that relationship. The gap between God and men opened up by our violation of God's law is simply unbridgeable by human effort. But God loves sinners and sent His only Son Jesus Christ to die on a cross for them. Sharon realised that Jesus Christ, as God and Saviour, was the only bridge across the gulf of sin. At last she repented and received the Lord Jesus Christ. She describes what happened:

"I prayed, 'Lord Jesus Christ, I confess that I have sinned against you. Please forgive me. I want you to be Lord and Saviour of my life. Amen'. It was then that Jesus Christ did what no other could do: He freed me. His Spirit filled the icy void...liberating me from the demons' grip...Instantly I knew that...Jesus Christ had saved me. It was finished...In that instant I also knew that the Bible was His voice and that I should give it authority over my desires, thoughts, feelings, and intuition...I was free...I sobbed my gratitude to Jesus. I cried my relief - I had found the Saviour of the World, Jesus Christ."

Since then Sharon has been free of all occult and spiritualistic chains and works as a licensed marriage and family therapist with her own Christian-based practice. Satan truly masquerades as an angel of light, peace, and goodness, yet as Sharon says: *"Nothing in New Age thinking or occult replicates the love of Christ, and underneath the sophisticated words and philosophies lies an empty heart and a vacant, cold, restless spirit; this can only be filled with God through repentance and faith in Jesus Christ as Lord and Saviour."*

CHAPTER 4

Saved Out Of Spiritualism

Jackie Lancaster

Remember those teenage years when sensation-seeking was a way of life? When I was 16 or 17, back in the 1970's, it became the 'in thing' to play with a ouija board. Once it was set up, my friends and I were aware that a 'power' had entered the room. Exciting and frightening, mirrors sometimes cracked, pictures fell off the wall and windows broke. We would scream, laugh and clutch onto one another all at the same time. None of us had the faintest idea what we were getting into, nor the reality behind the power being manifested.

I came from a wealthy, middle class family, went to a good school, and enjoyed the luxuries of life. Though attending a religious school (Christian Scientist), I had no proper concept of God. School assemblies meant little to me. The ouija board was much more interesting. The mischief that I and my School friends got into developed into a fascination with the occult. We acquired a book from somewhere which told us in detail how to conjure up manifestations. The cult films of Dennis Wheatly inspired us - indeed, all horror films fascinated us. We acquired black candles, masks, hoods and cloaks. It was all just a bit of harmless fun as far as we were concerned.

We discovered there was a witches' coven operating in an old ruined monastery in Surrey, south of London, so we went there to investigate the remains of rituals and ceremonies. Prior to that time I would never have believed what I saw there or what would happen in my life as a direct result of my involvement. The short-term result of my connection with the occult was depression and addiction to tranquillisers. I was also full of fear. I went to Art School, married and had a baby - but I was far from happy and basically lost in this world. Eventually my marriage broke up and I came from the country to live in London. I met some new faces and grew to know some interesting people who seemed contented and very much in control of their lives. I shared my sense of lostness with them and they encouraged me to join them at the local spiritualist church.

Among my new spiritualist friends, one was a highly trained graphologist and another a clairvoyant. Another became a close companion - she was so kind, she became like a surrogate mother to me. As I leaned on her for support my depression began to lift. There was light at the end of the tunnel after all. And then, suddenly she died, without warning. I was left feeling alone, angry and confused as to why God, if there was a God, seemed so determined to punish me.

I resolved to make a commitment to the spiritualist church. I went regularly to their meetings, mainly because I wanted to maintain contact with my dead friend. Controlling my future became a pet obsession. I listened avidly to any 'messages from the other side' that various mediums would have for me. Then, of course, there were the horoscopes, the tarot cards, the pendulums and the rune stones. I tried it all. Despite being already pretty messed up and confused, the worst was yet to come.

An elderly woman whom I looked up to as a kind of 'guru', told me that because there are so many people in the world, Jesus does not have enough time for them all. Therefore, what I needed was my own personal 'guide' -

someone to talk to. This guide would help me to aspire to greater levels of awareness. I accepted this spirit guide with open arms. Here at last was real help. How I relied on my guide! I soon did nothing without first consulting him. In reality my life had entered a state of captivity - I was chained to my guide and belonged to him without being fully aware of my position.

I was convinced that everything was alright because I was part of a 'Christian' spiritualist church. After all, I was privileged to be able to ask gifted 'healers' to lay their hands on me and heal me from a multitude of ailments. Occasionally I was healed, but the healing did not last. Spiritualism is a glamorous religion; it is visual and exciting. Dramatic things happen and people are easily drawn in via the readings, tarot cards and horoscopes. Once you are in, it becomes a way of life, a never-ending spiritual journey to masterhood. Now the spiritualist church recognises Jesus as one of the 'masters', but it also holds out the goal of mastery to each person willing to follow the right path. Belief in karma and good works to pay back karmic debt is extremely strong. One is constantly in the grip of having to pay back karmic debts by doing good works. Spiritualists do not recognise the Lord Jesus as the atoning sacrifice for the sins of others. I never remember the word 'sin' being mentioned in the meetings.

The crunch came when I and my 10-year-old daughter and a friend spent one thrilling evening reading tarot cards and swinging a pendulum. It all seemed so harmless. We were enjoying ourselves asking the pendulum, or rather the force behind it, to tell us what would happen in the future. We were oblivious to the danger we were courting. I will never forget what happened that night. My daughter, who had gone to bed peacefully, woke up screaming. She screamed and screamed - indescribably chilling screams. Still screaming, she rushed from her bedroom into the sitting room. I ran after her shouting *"Stop it,"* but to no avail.

She looked at me. My heart was pounding. The hairs stood up on the back of my neck. It was a horrible night of fear and terror. When calm returned the next day I asked her to explain to me what happened. She said that I had looked like the devil the night before. That was a turning point - from then on I knew had to get my daughter and myself out of spiritualism.

The night of the famous hurricane in the South West of England (October 1987) my cat died. That heralded a long bleak winter for me. The following March I remember so clearly going for a walk in the park, feeling very wretched, when a strange thing happened. It was as if I heard my name called out loudly, three times. I thought someone was with me, and I looked round, but there was no one there that I could see. Looking back now I believe it was God calling me to Himself. It was at that point that I turned from my sin and believed in the Lord Jesus Christ, receiving Him as my Lord and Saviour. Suddenly everything was different. I knew there was a personal God, who loved me and His name was Jesus. No longer was He just an ascended master, but the Son of God - God manifest in the flesh.

I cannot say that everything was a bed of roses from then on. I had a long battle trying to get out from the clutches of the Spiritualist Church. I had to have extensive prayer and counselling. I also had to burn everything which had any association with spiritualism. Today I know that both my daughter and I are brand new creations, that we are washed clean by the blood of Jesus. For the first time, I am completely happy and set free from fear. God also delivered me from my tranquillizer addiction, effortlessly and with no withdrawal. I now have a new purpose for my life and am assured that God is changing both my daughter and me into the image that He always planned for us. If you are involved in spiritualism I trust my short life story will be a blessing to you and that you too will come to know the Lord Jesus as He really is.

CHAPTER 5

The Beautiful Side of Evil

Johanna Michaelsen
California USA.

The tension was almost unbearable as we searched through the dark streets of Mexico City. We were lost. We were too late to witness any of the operations scheduled for that night. Kim, my sister, was leaving Mexico the next day. This had been my last chance to make her understand.

"This is it! We're here!"

Tom my companion exclaimed as he jerked the car into a parking space in front of an old market. We walked across the dark street to a grimy white metal gate, which swung open even as Tom knocked. We stepped into a narrow courtyard crowded with people, some obviously wealthy, others clothed in rags, but all drawn together by a common bond of suffering which reached out into the unknown for the healing denied them by conventional medicine.

We made our way through the crowd toward the entrance to the smelly operating room. The focal point of the room was a large tiered altar, covered with dozens of jars and vases crowded with rotten roses. A picture of Christ on the cross and a large wooden crucifix stood surrounded by white candles. Next to the crucifix, in the centre of the altar, was a bronze statue of *Cuauhtemoc*, the Aztec prince who had defiantly borne torture and death at the hands of Spanish *conquistadores.* At its feet lay a pair of surgical scissors and a rusty hunting knife.

My eyes turned to the right side of the room. There, on a cot, sat a wise old woman called Pachita, a psychic surgeon of phenomenal ability. A worn blanket was wrapped about her legs. Her hands were covered to the wrist in dry, crusted blood. I turned to look again at the altar. Waves of soft light now seemed to be coming from the image of the warrior and the crucifix beside it.

"Lord God," I whispered. "Thank You for this place. After all the years of terror You have now brought me into a temple of light. Let me serve You here, Lord."

My prayer was interrupted by the voice of a young man.

"Tell me what are you feeling?" he asked.

"I'm not sure," I answered softly. "I feel I'm in the presence of my God."

"Then you must touch the statue of Cuauhtemoc!" he exclaimed.

I hesitated, then reached out my hand and with my fingertips lightly touched the image of the ancient Aztec warrior who was now Pachita's spirit guide. At the third touch a light shock ran through my fingers. Everything grew still and silent. I was enveloped in a deep velvet peace, which wrapped itself around me like a mantle on the shoulders of a priest.

Pachita turned her tired face to me and focused on my eyes, staring through me with a frightening intensity. No word was spoken for many seconds. Then a blood-crusted hand reached out and pulled me closer.

"You're very sensitive...are you a medium?"

Her words startled me, and I hesitated.

"I...I'm not sure, Pachita," I answered. *"Sometimes I think so."*

"Well, my little one," she replied. *"You finish the studies in Mind Control you have begun with Tom and then return."*

Aunt Dixie was my mother's grandfather's sister. Most of the family had been frightened of her and her strange powers. She was famous in her time, with her picture appearing in the newspapers of Europe and America. She had extraordinary psychic abilities and was known as a spiritualist and effective trance medium. Sometime in the 1920's she died - alone, forgotten, and a pauper.

It wasn't until June 1975, two years after my experience with spiritualism was all over, that I learned of Aunt Dixie's prediction: someone in the third generation - my generation - was to inherit her talent.

The colony in which I grew up was located on the outskirts of Cuernavaca, 45 miles south of Mexico City. I was almost 12 years old when someone, or something, moved into that home. It happened late one night when Mum and Dad were away for a few hours. My sister, Kim, was asleep in her bed. I could see her from my room as I sat up reading. Suddenly, angry footsteps stormed down the hall. A door opened and slammed shut. Then another. Kim sat up, startled, and rubbed her eyes.

"Oh," she murmured sleepily. *"Mummy and Daddy are home,"* and fell back to sleep.

I got up and went into my parents' room to say

goodnight, but there was no one there. The rooms were empty. Suddenly I was afraid. I walked into the living room. I felt a dead, clammy chill as if I had stepped suddenly into a giant icebox filled with dead flesh. The presence of something evil permeated the air and I began to shiver. The front door was standing wide open. Dad had locked it twice before he left, but now it was standing open - yet there was no one in the house. I walked across the room and shut the door. Soft, low laughter began to echo in my head, a kind of laughter I had never heard before and which filled me with terror. The being that moved into our home that night seemed to take a grim delight in frightening me. Strange and morbid apparitions and voices haunted me for years to come, manifestations that increased and intensified during my college years.

When I was fourteen, Bishop Pike came to stay with us. In February 1966 the Bishop's son committed suicide and the Bishop started attending seances in order to contact his dead son.

"*Hey, Johanna, listen to this,*" my Father shouted up at me from his room where he was reading the newspaper. "*And I quote: 'The Silva Mind Control Method. In 48 hours you can learn to use your mind to do everything you wish. You can learn to overcome depression, relieve insomnia, eliminate negative thinking, avoid irrational fears* (my dad's deep theatre voice gave this last point special emphasis), *relieve nervousness, develop ESP, and even gain peace of mind!' Sounds like something right up your alley, dear.*"

"What it sounds is bizarre," I said, coming into the room. "Probably some bunch of weirdos."

"More than likely," Dad agreed. "But at least it would give you something to do."

He had a point there. I was depressed, lonely and

bored since my return to Mexico after graduation from college in the United States.

"They're having an introductory meeting tonight. Why don't you and Mother go."

We went. The promises listed in the ad were confirmed and embellished at the introductory meeting by a confident-looking man in his mid-30s named Tom. He explained about the various brain-wave frequencies and assured us there was virtually nothing a controlled mind couldn't do, from developing genius potential to overcoming bad habits. We would even learn to heal diseases in much the same fashion as the famed psychic Edgar Cayce, the main difference being that we would learn to do it in a conscious state. Tom also told us about a wonderful old woman named Pachita and about the incredible operations she performed. The first time he met her, she had sliced open his knee and repaired an old football injury. The knee had not bothered him since. Mother and I signed up.

I gave myself joyously to the sessions, believing that Mind Control was my salvation indeed! On the third day of the course we learned to project our minds psychically into metals, leaves, and little animals.

"It all might, at this stage, appear to be imaginary to some of you," Tom pointed out. "But very real things are taking place on a different dimension. Trust me."

I had long been aware of that other dimension and it had terrorised me for years. It was incredible to discover that there was a beautiful and positive side to psychic phenomena! On the fourth day, we met our spirit guides. Silva Mind Control prefers the term 'counsellors'. I knew immediately I wanted Jesus as my only counsellor, but since we were told we had to have a female as well, I opted for Sarah Bernhardt. That night, however, both Sarah and Jesus manifested themselves as hideous werewolves. Fresh blood was smeared on their muzzles and matted hair, and yet a shimmering radiance still surrounded them.

"*Do not be afraid,*" I was told, as I watched the faces of Jesus and Sarah interchange with the horrible apparitions. "*We only want to teach you that not everything that seems to be evil on the surface really is evil down beneath in its essence.*"

The message was clear: if an apparition appeared evil, it was just my lack of spiritual growth that made it appear so. Within weeks of this, Sarah announced she was no longer to be my counsellor and left. Seconds later, a small Mexican Indian woman materialised in my mind. Her eyes were deep amber in colour, her face chiselled, but beautiful. She was dressed in a servant's garb.

"*You are to call me Mamacita* (Little Mother)," she announced. "*I have come to remind you of your coming role as servant. I will teach you humility and lead you into true wisdom.*"

I knew with her arrival that the time had come for me to meet Pachita. The six days following my first meeting with Pachita, recounted earlier, were spent in deep mental and spiritual preparation. I sensed I was on the brink of my life's work and ultimate fulfilment in my search for God. I knew the years of fear were over; my spirit guides, Jesus and Mamacita, were with me, teaching me to overcome the lower spiritual entities.

On Friday, July 27, 1971, the morning of the seventh day, I returned to see Pachita. I arrived around 11:30 in the morning. The courtyard was already crowded with people waiting to see *Hermanito Cuauhtemoc* (that is, 'Little Brother', as the spirit who worked through Pachita was affectionately called). Each person in line was instructed to have a fresh raw egg to present to Hermanito for the spiritual limpia (cleansing). When my turn finally came, I stood before Hermanito, holding the egg in my hand. He placed both hands on my shoulders and, in a voice much deeper and gruffer than Pachita's own, commanded;

"*To work, my little daughter.*"

"*How do I begin, Hermanito?*"

Hermanito nodded towards Memo, Pachita's oldest son, who was sitting on the cot.

"*The son of my flesh will give you instructions.*" (Hermanito always spoke of Pachita in the third person calling her 'my flesh').

Memo said:

"*Hermanito is telling you that you will work as a full-trance medium - that you will one day heal as my mother does. You are to begin preparing immediately. Come back this Monday. Hermanito himself will tell you what you must do.*"

I returned as instructed the following Monday night. The rain pelted down on the tin roof of the altar room. A candle was lit and placed upon the altar. The single naked light bulb was switched off. Pachita put on Hermanito's satin robe and sat on the straight-back wooden chair in front of the altar. She told us to gather around and pray. She closed her eyes, placed her hands straight and stiff on her spread knees, and began taking deep breaths. The atmosphere in the room seemed to thicken as a powerful unseen presence descended upon Pachita. Suddenly her body quivered violently. Her right hand raised in a sharp, straight-armed salute and a deeper, stronger voice than hers announced:

"*I am with you, beloved brothers.*" Hermanito arose and directed a nervous well-dressed woman named Rita to sit in the chair. *"Keep praying, my little ones,"* Hermanito said. *"Only with God's help will we be able to heal this woman's eye."*

Chalio, a young engineer who frequently assisted Hermanito, stood behind Rita. He had cut large strips of cotton from the roll Rita's husband had brought. Smaller patches were placed in a small bowl and alcohol was poured over them, Hermanito's one concession to physical antiseptics. Hermanito called me to his side.

"Come, little daughter, you will help me."

He instructed me to hold a large block of cotton under Rita's chin. *"Rita,"* Hermanito said. *"I want you to sit very still now. Keep your eyes open and looking up at the ceiling. Do you understand me, little one?"*

"Is it going to hurt me, Hermanito?" she asked, her voice quivering.

"No, little one, you are even now being anaesthetised," Hermanito said reassuringly.

He took the new bottle of alcohol I was holding, opened it, and poured it directly into her eye. I gasped, expecting the woman to cry out, but she just sat there. Then Hermanito sprinkled some of the balsam on the eye.

"Very well, little one, now hand me the cotton you have there."

As I handed him the smaller cotton strips, he formed a square leaving the eye exposed in the centre. Then he asked for the scissors and the old knife that lay on the altar. Hermanito took the scissors and raised them in a salute toward the altar as he began a prayer in the ancient Aztec language. As he prayed, I saw that the area where we stood, and especially around Rita's head, became much brighter than the rest of the room, as though a soft spotlight were shining down on us. I was to witness this phenomenon at each of the several hundred operations in which I assisted in the coming months.

"Pray to God, little ones!"

Hermanito pushed one point of the scissors into Rita's eye and began to cut. A pale reddish-white liquid trickled into a piece of cotton that fell off her face and dropped onto her chest. I caught it and replaced it, my face only inches from her eye.

"Do you feel pain, little one?" he asked her.

"No, Hermanito," Rita answered.

He began peeling a thin opaque scum off the centre of the eye. It broke. He placed the first piece on the cotton I held out; then he gently lifted off the second part of the tissue and handed it to me. Again he poured alcohol into the eye, then placed a clean pad of cotton over it. When the job of bandaging was done, he instructed two men to wrap Rita in a sheet and carry her across the courtyard to rest in the house. The entire procedure had taken perhaps 15 minutes. A week later I learned that Rita's operation at the hospital had been cancelled. The doctors were astonished at the total disappearance of the cataract. Rita's operation was the first operation I had ever seen Hermanito perform. It was on that night that he gave me instructions and meditations for becoming a full-trance medium, even as Pachita was. She had been working with Hermanito for 46 years at that point.

"Hermanito has performed marvellous healings through me," she later told me, *"but I don't know for how much longer. I am old and tired. My sons have refused my mantle. They are too busy with their own things to sacrifice themselves in this*

work. It will fall to you, little one, for you are gifted and willing. I will teach you all I know."

I made the trip across the mountains into Mexico City at least once or twice a week, sometimes more, to be with Pachita and to assist during the consultations and operations. I saw incredible things - things that defy belief.

After one particularly miraculous day I lay in bed at night thinking about the things I had seen. Was it possible that it had all been a trick? Had it all been sleight of hand and a fraud? Had I been hypnotized? I saw things that I believed were medically impossible. But my face was only inches from the action. And I had a clear view of Pachita's hands, which were open, fingers spread. Nothing was palmed in them. At no time did she pull anything out from under her tunic. And I had felt the warm blood pulse over my hands. My hands were in the wound - blood was smeared to my wrists from it. But what she did was impossible!

The being working through Pachita was clearly not human. He was supernatural - he was beyond the realm of physical laws as we know them, and so the effect and works which he performed were also supernatural and not bound by conventional rules.

The spirits are right then, I thought to myself. My sister, Kim, was wrong. This work of Pachita's was not satanic. How could it be? Was there not a crucifix on the altar and a picture of Jesus? I had seen nuns and priests there, sprinkling holy water throughout the room and reciting the rosary. All glory was given to 'My Father and Lord'; we were constantly told to elevate our thoughts to God and to say the Lord's Prayer. Besides, what purpose would Satan have in healing and doing good works? No, there was no question in my mind that what Pachita did found its ultimate source in God. I was therefore determined that I should work there to learn and serve as best I could. I praised God again and again for having led me there.

By September 1972 I had been working, with Pachita for over 14 months. I had washed the blood of over 200 operations from my hands. I had seen everything from the removal of brain tumours to lung transplants. I had seen things materialise and removed from the human body during *dano* (curse) operations which further defied belief and logical explanation.

Despite all I had learned in the last year, I was not a full-trance medium as Hermanito had said I would be. I was not developing as I should, as I knew Hermanito had expected me to. He had said nothing to me about my failure, but I could sense his disappointment and I felt vaguely ashamed and uneasy.

But there were other things that troubled me. I was finding that some cures Hermanito performed were only temporary. I also couldn't understand why Hermanito treated Pachita so cruelly - never allowing her any new or pretty clothes, and refusing to treat her when she was sick. And her family was falling apart around her. Over the months, what peace I had perceived there deteriorated in the presence of almost constant tension and bickering among her children.

Things had become hectic. The vision was no longer clear as it had seemed when I first arrived. I needed to get away for a while, to spend time alone where I could commune with God and find my way again. For six weeks I wandered around England. Eventually I found my way to Florence, Italy, to see my sister, who had been living there for several months since her graduation from college that summer.

Quite frankly, I had mixed emotions about visiting her. As a committed Christian, Kim was certain all my pet activities, namely yoga (I had been teaching hatha yoga and learning raja yoga for about a year), Mind Control, and psychic surgery, were 'of the devil', and said so. I was equally assured of the fact that she, on the other hand, was a narrow-minded, bigoted, Bible-thumping evangelical, who wouldn't know a genuine miracle from God if it ran her over in the street. After all, I had spent much of my life terrorised by evil beings. I *knew* what their source was. But now, through meditation, Pachita, and my counsellors, I was seeing wonderful things, miraculous operations, hope restored, evil spirits cast out. Granted, there were a few discrepancies I couldn't explain, but nevertheless Satan couldn't heal, could he?

I had been in Florence with Kim for only a few days when, not altogether unexpectedly, the general thread of this conversation was soon picked up and we were off again. This time, however, Kim's tactics took a slightly different bent. She asked questions - questions which now began echoing some of my own hidden doubts.

"You say you can tell the difference between good and evil spirits, but how can you be sure your senses haven't been deceived? Yes, Pachita performs amazing operations, but how do you know for sure her source of power is God? You say you believe in Jesus - but which one? How do you know the Jesus you see is the Jesus of the Bible? How do you know demons are truly being cast out? It is possible that they are just playacting?"

I had to admit, if only to myself, I didn't really know. The only argument I could fall back on was my experience - my feelings and perceptions. Yes, I had read and studied masters like Edgar Cayce and others. I could give eloquent explanations when asked about reincarnation, karma and cosmic consciousness, astral planes and psychic manifestations. But when it came right down to it, I knew there was no solid, truly objective way of testing the source behind them, and that troubled me. How *could* I be sure the source was God? I had no absolutes against which to compare my experience. For the first time I sat still and quiet under the gentle but insistent onslaught of Kim. She stopped and took my hand.

"Johanna, why don't you go to L'Abri in Switzerland for a few days? Os Guinness is a counsellor there - he knows a lot about these things. Maybe he can help make all this clearer to you."

I looked up sharply. L'Abri! I knew that L'Abri was a place of Christian ministry founded by Francis and Edith Schaeffer. It was the last place in the world I wanted to go.

"Don't look so distressed," Kim laughed. "I'm not asking you to move in permanently; just go for a couple of days and talk to Os. It can't hurt to listen. Besides, your train goes near the place on your way back to England anyway."

I took a deep breath. "All right. I'll go. Who knows? Maybe there is something for me there."

To my relief, the image I had of dozens of fire and brimstoners trying to convert me on my arrival at L'Abri never materialised. After several days of relatively peaceful anonymity, I decided to talk to Os and Sheila Bird (the counsellor with whom Kim had suggested I spend time before seeing Os). Sunday morning, after chapel, I had someone point 'Birdie' out to me. She was a small woman probably in her 40's. I watched Birdie's face as she spoke with a young girl. Her eyes were stern, but kind. As I moved closer, Birdie glanced over at me and stopped in mid-sentence.

"You must be Kim's sister!" she exclaimed. I nodded. "Kim called several days ago. Os and I have been expecting you. Why don't you come by my chalet after lunch today for a visit?"

When I arrived at her chalet, Birdie ushered me into a tiny, cosy room and finally, after much gentle coaxing, had me talking about the beings and manifestations that filled my life. She was silent for several minutes after I had finished.

"Well, Johanna, I can certainly see why you believe as you do, but something about what Pachita is doing makes me uncomfortable. Let's not talk about it just now, though. First I'd like you to spend the next day or so reading the Gospel of John and the first epistle of John. It will help lay a foundation for our next meeting."

It seemed a reasonable request. I had read I John and the Gospels several times in the past, but the words never had the same impact on me that they had now. The Jesus I was encountering on the pages of that Bible was not only alive and real, but was filled with awesome power and majesty. A mere spoken word of healing or deliverance was sufficient to bring it about. His claim to unique incarnate deity was unmistakable despite what I still believed about it. Verse after verse asserted that apart from Him there was no forgiveness of sin.

I was shaken and confused by the time I finished the last verse in the Gospel of John. If what I had just read was true, then everything I believed about karma and the way to unity with God was wrong. It couldn't be both ways. The claims made by Jesus were too exclusive. And if I was wrong about what I believed about Jesus, then maybe I was wrong about the rest as well.

Despite a well-rehearsed, serene exterior, I was in turmoil by the time I arrived at Os Guinness' home to talk with him about the eastern aspects of my belief system. Part of me wanted desperately to know the truth, another part of me still wanted to shut down and ignore the whole business. Os spoke to me about the irreconcilable gulf between the Eastern and the biblical view of God, salvation, and Jesus.

While I had always believed that Hinduism and

Christianity were fully compatible (Swami Vivekenanda had said, *"We accept all religions as true"*), Os emphasised that, far from compatible, the two philosophies were radically opposed to one another in their basic concepts of God, reality, morality, and personality. He pointed out that although several gurus taught that the teachings of 'the Blessed Lord Jesus Christ' dovetailed perfectly with Hinduism, their claim lacked scholastic integrity. These gurus, Os continued, lifted phrases such as 'The Kingdom of Heaven is within you' out of context and blatantly ignored other less pliable statements such as *"I am the way, and the truth, and the life; no one comes to the Father, but by me"* (John 14:6). This point especially caught my attention, as this had been one of the sayings of Jesus with which I myself had long struggled and had sought to explain away. It was too intolerant a statement, too narrow-minded to possibly be anything other than a misinterpretation or mistranslation of the Bible. Yet the first epistle and the gospel of John were filled with such statements. Here is a sample verse from each book:

"I said therefore to you, that you shall die in your sins; for unless you believe that I am He, you shall die in your sins." (John 8:24)...*"And the witness is this, that God has given us eternal life, and this life is in His Son. He who has the Son has life; he who does not have the Son of God does not have life."* (1 John 5:11-12)

Os summarised his discussion by saying:

"If treated fairly on its own premises, Christianity excludes the full truth and final validity of other religions. If Christianity is true, Hinduism cannot be true in the sense it claims. Even though on the surface it appears that Hinduism is more tolerant, both finally demand an ultimate choice."

Intellectually, Os' discussion made sense to me. Spiritually, however, I couldn't accept it. I felt torn between two powerful, relentless forces. The pressure finally drove me to my knees. I again challenged God to show me, once and for all, the truth. Was Jesus the greatest avatar, the way-shower; or perhaps the greatest creation of Father God; or was He God uniquely incarnate in human flesh who died to take away my sin, as the Gospel of John and Os and Birdie and Kim claimed? Was Pachita working in the power of God or was her source satanic?

"If You can, God, show me now. I'm willing to give up Pachita and yoga and all the rest if I'm wrong. But if not, then I'm putting this entire nonsense aside and going on with it at Pachita's. Oh God, let me see the truth!"

I had no idea how literally God would answer that prayer. The night of November 15, 1972 was damp and cold as I walked alone on the slippery path to Birdie's chalet. A dense, black fog was forming all around, blotting out the path. Within seconds I could see nothing. The dark mist was swirling, alive, filled with the presence of something more monstrous than anything I had ever before encountered. Voices began whispering, hissing incoherent words and laughter in my right ear. An ice-cold breath touched the back of my neck under my hair.

"Hermanito, help me!" I gasped.

The voices shrieked in hideous laughter.

"We're going to kill you!"

I panicked and broke into a run. Something like a giant fist slammed into my back. I pitched forward in the darkness and reached out to break my fall. My fingers found the branch of a small bush and clung to it. I tried to scream out *"Jesus!"* but a hand closed upon my throat, choking me. I screamed in my mind *"Jesus, Jesus, help me!"*

"He can't help you," the voices shrieked. *"He can't help you!"*

But then suddenly the grip around my throat loosened - the blackness lifted. I could again see the light of Birdie's chalet at the end of the path. Birdie's eyes widened a little as I burst into the room.

"*What on earth is the matter with you!*" she exclaimed.

"*I don't know, Birdie,*" I said, still shaking, "*but I'm terrified.*"

Birdie hurried me into her little prayer room and closed the door. She took my hands in hers and began praying. I tried to focus on her words, but suddenly they sounded so far away. I felt dizzy. My eyes opened. The room seemed to have been taken up in a giant slow-motion whirlwind, spinning slowly round and around. The sound of voices began to build again. I turned my head toward the dark window on my left and froze. Outside I could see the faces of demons, contorted in indescribable rage.

"*What is it, Johanna?*" Birdie's voice sounded muffled.

"*Can't you see them, Birdie?* " I gasped. "*No,*" she said, "*but I know One who can. Satan, in the name of Jesus Christ of Nazareth, I command you to go! I forbid your presence here. I claim the protection of Jesus' blood upon us. Go where Jesus sends you!* "

Instantly the faces vanished. The room stopped spinning and was filled with a peace beyond all my understanding. They were gone. I knew what had happened was a direct answer to my prayer. God had literally let me see the source behind my practices. Murderous demonic rage had been the spirit's reaction to my potential repentant decision to receive Jesus Christ of Nazareth *as He is*, rather than as I had come to think He should be. The difference had been subtle, but vast nonetheless. There were still so many things I didn't understand, but I knew beyond any doubt that I had been wrong about Jesus. Two days later, Friday November

17, 1972 at 10 a.m. Os and Birdie supported me in prayer as I renounced my sinful involvement with the occult (repentance) and committed myself in absolute faith to Jesus Christ as my Lord and Saviour. I would never again face the darkness alone.

I have not written this story as an exercise in narcissistic morbidity. Writing the account of my life - reliving those days of darkness - has been one of the most difficult things I have ever done. Nor have I written my story to glorify the deeds of darkness. I have shared my story because of the times in which we live. Those of you who are, or have been, in the occult, and are seeking a way out of the darkness, will understand the relevance of my story. I have learned some basic principles from my many years of hard study and personal experience concerning the discernment of false prophets and healers, and the means of freedom from occultic involvement. Jesus in Matthew 24:24 said:

"For false Christs and false prophets will arise and will show great signs and wonders."

Revelation 16:14 speaks of the *"spirits of demons, performing signs,"* and the Bible elsewhere states that the antichrist, when he is revealed, will perform *"great signs, so that he even makes fire come down out of heaven to the earth in the presence of men"* (Revelation 13:13).

Demonic miracles *do* take place. The question that must be asked is not just did a genuine miracle occur, but what is the source behind it? How can we be certain if a healing or a miracle is from God? Here are five tests to help us distinguish the true prophets from the false. It is important to use *all* these tests, not just one or two.

1. *What does the prophet (or healer) believe about Jesus?*
Does he cling to Jesus Christ of Nazareth as the Son of God, equal with God, God incarnate in human flesh; who

died upon the cross in our place for the forgiveness of our sins; who was born of a virgin and whose physical resurrection from the dead proclaimed His victory over sin, death, and Satan? Or has he, through a subtle redefinition, come to accept 'another Jesus'. In Deuteronomy 13:1-5 the Lord states clearly that even if a prophet or a dreamer of dreams works genuine miracles, if he in any way seeks to lead you into trusting in another god, you are not to listen to him *"for the Lord your God is testing you to find out if you love the Lord your God with all your heart and with all your soul."*

2. *A prophet must be 100% accurate 100% of the time.*

The world's most famous prophets, as perhaps you've noticed, have a tendency toward inaccuracy. From Nostradamus to Jeane Dixon the failed prophecies are staggering! It should be obvious that if God were the source of their prophecies their words would be error free. The Bible says: *"When a prophet speaks in the name of the Lord, if the thing does not come about or come true, that is the thing which the Lord has not spoken. The prophet has spoken it presumptuously; you shall not be afraid of him"* (Deut 18:22).

3. *If a miracle, sign, prophecy or healing is performed by an occultist, or by means of occultic techniques, it is not from God. It is counterfeit.*

God made his position on the occult remarkably clear in Deuteronomy 18:9-14, where He lists the full gamut of occult categories, from superstition and channelling to child sacrifice, and flatly labels them all *detestable* (the King James Version uses the word *abominable)*. In case we missed it the first time around, He repeats it three times (in verse 9 and twice in verse 12). God knows the demonic source behind these practices and does not want people to be contaminated by them (Leviticus 19:31). God spoke through His prophets by dreams and visions, but not accompanied by occultic techniques. Now, granted, a false prophet may receive dreams and visions without using techniques of divination such as crystal balls, tarot cards, ouija boards, astrology and tea leaf reading. That is why *all* these tests must be applied. No single test, in and of itself, is sufficient. A false prophet or wonder-worker might pass one or two of these tests yet still be speaking lies and producing counterfeits.

4. *The test of the fruit of life must also be applied.*

While the lives of false prophets are sometimes above reproach, they are often characterised by a rebellious, unrepentant spirit. Matthew 7:15-23 is a key passage here. The Bible warns us against the false prophets *"who come to you in sheep's clothing, but inwardly are ravenous wolves"* (verse 15). How will we spot them? *"You will know them by their fruits"* (verse 16). The Bible then goes on to declare that these miracle working prophets never knew God and will be cast out on the day of judgment (verses 21-23).

5. *The final test is that of our subjective inner witness.*

When we walk in fellowship with the Lord, as we come to know Him, His Holy Spirit bears witness within us concerning these things. But where we have grieved His Holy Spirit through sin and disobedience, this inner witness becomes warped and distorted and we no longer see or understand. Our inner witness may no longer be accurate. The Lord said:

"If any man is willing to do His will, he shall know of the teaching, whether it is of God, or whether I speak from Myself" (John 7:17).

If we truly want to know the truth and are willing to be obedient to it, God will make it evident within us. Sadly, too many of us insist our inner witness is the first and most important criterion. It is not. The most vital test is to bring our beliefs and experiences to the Bible and compare notes. May God bless you as you search for Him.

CHAPTER 6

For The Reader

It may be that you have identified with the life stories in this booklet. In the course of your search perhaps you've tried some or all of the experiences retold here. The fact of the matter is that spirit guides, channelling, psychic readings and healing therapies will not bring you closer to God or the truth. There is something in your life actively preventing such a breakthrough. Back in the beginning a perfect relationship existed between man and God. The world that God created was perfect and Adam and Eve were sinless beings.

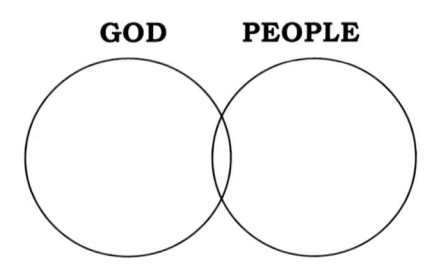

However, our first parents rebelled, broke God's law and went their own way. The human race they fathered has lived in a state of alienation from God ever since. Like Adam and Eve you too have broken God's laws and therefore, in the words of the Bible: *"Your iniquities* [wrongdoings] *have separated between you and your God"* (Isa 59:2).

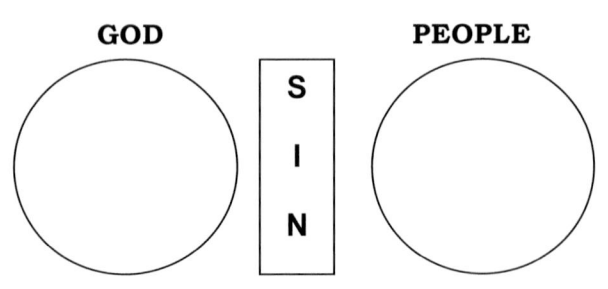

God's law says, *'Thou shalt not take the name of the Lord Thy God in vain'*. Have you ever said 'Jesus' or 'Christ' as a substitute for a four-letter swear word? Then you've broken this commandment. God's law also says, *'Thou shalt not commit adultery'*. The Bible says in another place that just looking at a woman lustfully is committing adultery in your heart! Who can claim to be free of guilt on this score? God's law says, *'Thou shalt not bear false witness'*. To 'bear false witness' means to tell lies. Have you ever done that? Why, of course, you say, everyone has. That condemns us all as liars.

Furthermore, the Bible says that on judgment day God is going to *'judge the secrets of men'* (Romans 2:16). Think about that. Not only will you face the music for breaking God's laws; He is also going public with all your secrets. When this happens, do you think you will be declared innocent or guilty by the judge of the universe? If you have faced these facts honestly, your conscience has already agreed with God and owned its guilt. You stand condemned by your own thoughts, words and deeds. Now ask yourself this question; what will my destiny be for eternity, heaven or hell?

At this point, many people, having realised they have broken God's laws and are facing judgment, start trying to merit God's favour by all kinds of good works and religious activity. They hope that on judgment day God will balance their good deeds against their bad deeds and let them into heaven. They think that God is so good and loving, He'll just forgive and forget. But, think about it this way. A man is in Court for serious fraud. As the judge is about to sentence him, the guilty man says, *"Wait! You've forgotten about all the good things I did and how religious I was. Besides, you are too good to condemn me."* No. A crime is a crime. It has to be paid for; so the judge fines the man £50,000. The law demands it.

In the same way, God's law demands the death penalty on your law breaking (sin). God's prison for guilty sinners is hell. And it goes on forever. Hell is a place you want to avoid at all costs. The situation looks hopeless doesn't it? You're basically doomed. But wait! Let's go back to the courtroom. Imagine if the judge offered to pay the fine: that would free the criminal from the demands of the law wouldn't it, providing he was willing to accept the payment?

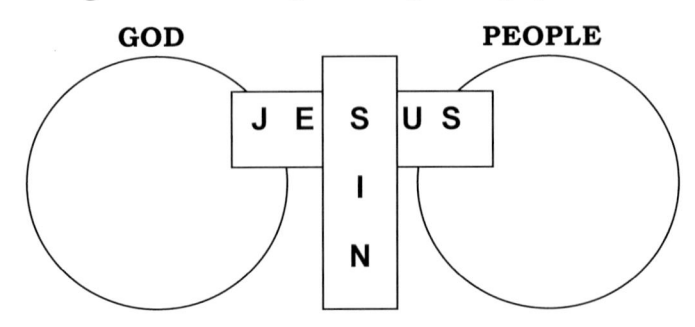

```
        GOD              PEOPLE
         ___    ┌───────────┐   ___
        /   \   │ J E  S U S│  /   \
       │     ├──┤           ├─┤     │
        \___/   │     I     │  \___/
                │     N     │
                └───────────┘
```

In Romans 5:6 the Bible says *"Christ died for the ungodly."* Had he broken God's law? No. Did he have any secret sins? No. Why then, did He die? Verse 8 continues: *"But God commends His love toward us in that while we were yet sinners, Christ died for us."* Do you see what the Bible is saying? God loved you so much that He sent His Son, the Lord Jesus, to pay your fine. Jesus died in the place of guilty hell-deserving sinners. No one but Christ could have done that, because only He is the sinless Son of God.

If you have a proper sense of the dreadfulness of your sin against a holy God and you are willing to turn from that sin, God wants you to know that His Son, the Lord Jesus Christ, died for guilty sinners on the cross. Can you not see how Christ's death on the cross meets the demands of God against your sin? If you understand who Christ is and what He has done, repent and believe in Him at once. John 3:36 says, *"He who believes on the Son [Jesus] has everlasting life: and he who believes not the Son shall not see life, but the wrath of God abides on him."* Don't trust religion or good works: trust Christ at once.

If you have repented and trusted Christ as your Lord and Saviour you should immediately take the following steps:

1. Thank Him for what He has done for you and ask yourself the question, "What can I now do for Him."

2. Start speaking daily to Him in prayer from your heart, bringing Him praise and thanksgiving, as well as asking Him for blessings.

3. Get a Bible and start reading and studying it. It's best to begin with the Gospels (e.g. Mark or John) and read through the New Testament. Ask God to give you understanding on how to apply it practically to your life.

4. Find a Bible believing Church and attend its meetings every week.

5. Tell others what the Lord has done for you.

If you would like confidential help or further information, please feel free to contact us. We can supply free Christian literature and addresses of Bible believing churches in your area.

If this book has been a help to you please let us know.
We greatly value the feedback we receive from our readers.

Acknowledgements:
Seance Fever
Kind permission of Gospel Tract Distributors, Portland OR U.S.A.
Set Free
Compiled from a cassette recording of Sadie Bryce telling her own life story and with the kind permission of her daughter Helena. (Sadie Bryce died in April 1999)
Enticed by the Light
Condensed version of *Enticed By The Light* by Sharon Beekmann. Copyright 1997 by Sharon Beekmann. Used by permission of Zondervan Publishing House.
Saved out of Spiritualism
Kind permission of Reachout Trust, Richmond, Surrey, England.
The Beautiful Side of Evil
Kind permission of Harvest House Publishers, Eugene, OR USA.

Also available:

Dawn of the New Age	5 New Agers Relate Their Search for the Truth
Light Seekers	5 Hindus Search for God
The Pilgrimage	5 Muslims Make the Greatest Discovery
Witches and Wizards	5 Witches Find Eternal Wisdom
The Evolution Crisis	5 Evolutionists Think Again
They Thought they were Saved	5 Christians Recall a Startling Discovery
Messiah	5 Jewish People Make the Greatest Discovery

Available from bookshops or direct from the publishers.

Published by:
John Ritchie Ltd.
40 Beansburn, Kilmarnock, Ayrshire, KA3 1RL.
Tel: + 44 (0) 1563 536394
Fax: + 44 (0) 1563 571191
Email: sales@johnritchie.co.uk
Web: www.ritchiechristianmedia.co.uk

Copyright: John Ritchie Ltd., 2011
ISBN: 978-1-907731-42-6